Let's Start Learning
PHONICS

Original Title: Letters and Sounds

by Dina Anastasio
cover illustration by Bari Weissman
illustrated by Theresa Fitzgerald

Scholastic Get Set Learning Skills Books are designed to help children understand that words are made up of sounds — and letters representing those sounds. Children are asked to add letters to make words they know, to read and to write whole words, and to use words to complete sentences. *Let's Start Learning Phonics* provides a comprehensive review of beginning and ending consonant blends and diagraphs and introduces long vowel sounds. The lively stickers and varied activities reinforce these basic phonics skills in a way that makes learning fun.

SCHOLASTIC INC.
New York Toronto London Auckland Sydney

TO THE PARENT:

- Set aside a special time and place to work with your child. Your interest communicates that reading is both valuable and enjoyable.
- Make sure the directions on each page are clear to your child.
- Read aloud the title on the top of each page and ask your child to read it again with you. Encourage your child's verbal participation as much as possible. Extend activities by having your child say other words that have the same sounds as the ones you are working with on a particular page.
- Be sensitive to the pace at which your child works and learns. Remember that some pages may be a lot of work and can be completed at another time.
- Reward good work with praise and liberal use of reward stickers.

Your involvement in the learning process will help your child GET SET to read!

STICKER INSTRUCTIONS

Carefully punch out stickers.
Moisten them and put on pages where they belong.

Rewards!
Use these stickers on any page.

ISBN 0-590-45272-X

Copyright © 1988 by Scholastic Inc.
All rights reserved. Published by Scholastic Inc.

12 11 10 9 8 7 6 5 4 3 2 1   10   2 3 4 5 6 7/9
Printed in the U.S.A.

sl

sloth sled

Read the title aloud.
The two letters together make one special sound.
Say the first sound in the word **sled.**
Write:

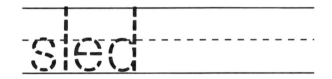

Sloths are slow animals.
The sloths have lost their slippers.
Help the sloths by drawing a line from each sloth to
his missing slipper.

sleepy sloth

slipper

One sloth is still missing his slipper.
Find it on the sticker page.
Put it with the other slippers.

 **ch** **chicken**
chair

Read the title aloud.
Say the first sound in the word **chicken.**
Write:

chicken

Color the pictures for words that start with the same
sound as the word chicken.

tree   chicken   church

cheese   child

wagon

flower

Write **ch** to complete each word. Read each word.

___erry   ___in   ___ain   ___air

One picture in each row starts with the **ch** sound.
Draw a circle around it.
Then write **ch** to complete each word. Read each word.

car   child   kite   shoe   ___ild

cake   dog   chair   sun   ___air

nest   chick   coat   cat   ___ick

What does a chick say?
Find the word on the sticker page, and put the
sticker here:

 **sh** **sheep shell**

Read the title aloud.
Say the first sound in the word **sheep.**
Write:

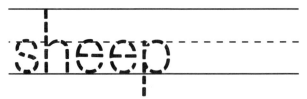

Two of the sheep in the picture are exactly the same.
Draw a circle around each of them.

sheep shouting   sheep sharing

shirt

shoe

sheep   sheep shivering

Find a sheep's shadow on the sticker page. Put it behind one of the sheep.

Write **sh** to complete each word. Say the word.

___ip   ___ark   ___adow   ___ow

Cross out all of the things on this page that *do not* begin with **sh.**

sheep

wheel

shark

stamp

cup

sheet

shadow

moon

shell

box

shelf

bear

Skill: sound/symbol relationship for sh

th

thimble
thumb

Read the title aloud.
Say the first sound in the word **thumb.**
Write:

thumb

Find thirteen thimbles in the picture.
Draw a circle around each thimble as you find it.

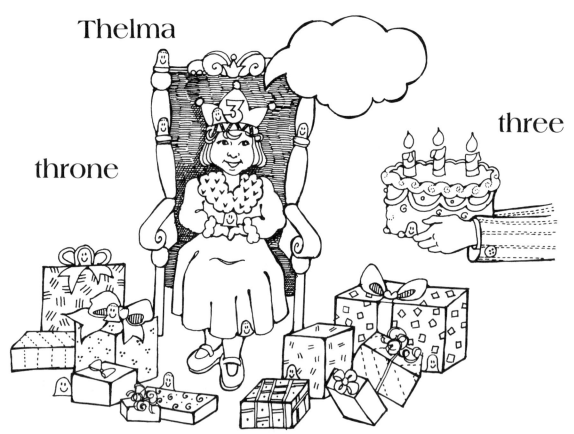

Thelma

three

throne

What does Thelma say when she receives a birthday gift?
Find the word on the sticker page and put it in the balloon.

Use these words to finish the puzzle.

→ thimble
   thirteen

↓ thirty
   thumb

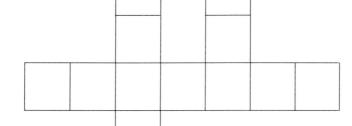

Sk skunk ski

Read the title aloud.
Say the first sound in the word **skunk.**
Write:

skunk

The skunk skis down the hill. Find the path to the house.

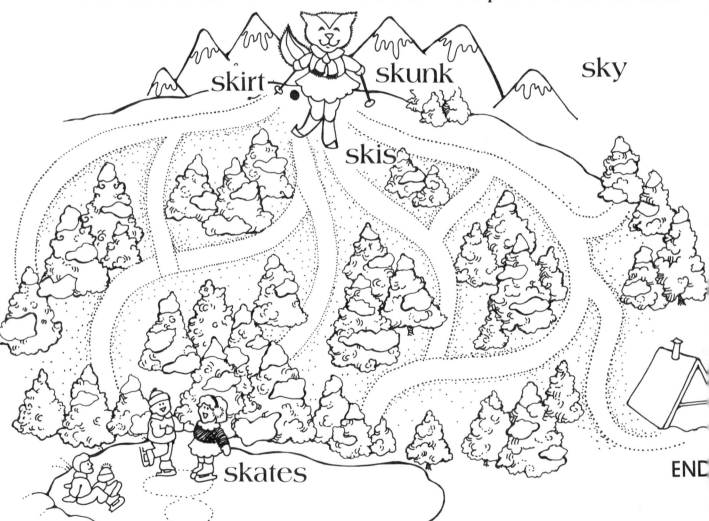

skirt   skunk   sky

skis

skates

END

Find a skating skunk on the sticker page. Put it in the picture.

10

Write **sk** on the lines to complete the words.
Draw a line from each word to the matching picture.

___irt

___unk

___ate

Find this sticker.

___is

bl

block
blanket

Read the title aloud.
Say the first sound in the word **block.**
Write:

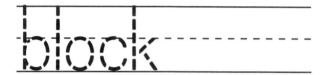

block

Find four birds in the picture below.
Color the two blackbirds black.
Color the two bluebirds blue.

blackbirds

bluebirds

blanket

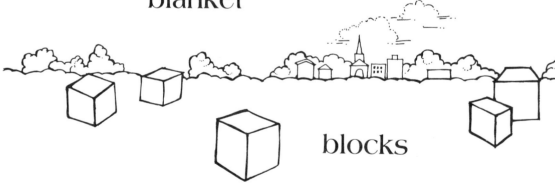

blocks

Write **bl** on each line to complete the words.
Read the sentences.

The _____ue _____anket is _____owing.

The _____ocks are _____ack and _____ue.

The _____ossom is _____ooming.

Use a blue crayon to color all the words that start with the same sound as the word **blouse**.
Did you make a blue blob?
Find the words BLUE BLOB on the sticker page.

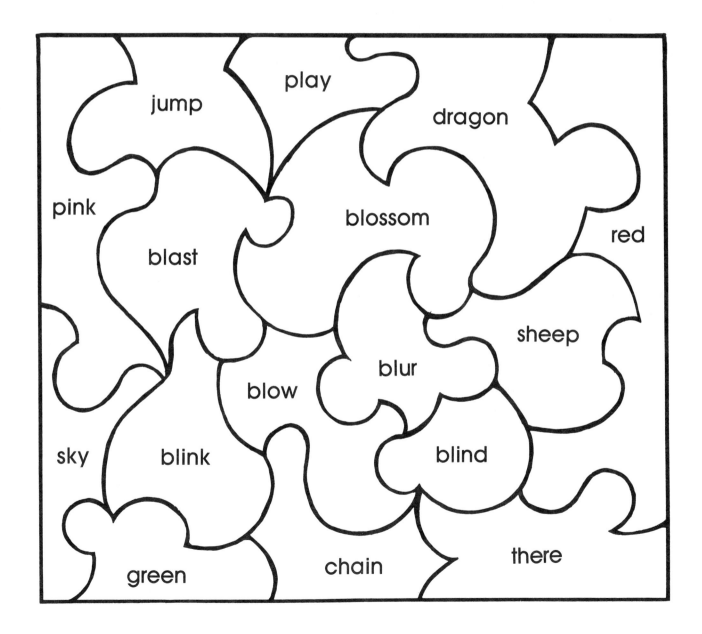

 **fl**

flower fly

Read the title aloud.
Say the first sound in the word **flower.**
Write:

Put these pictures in order.
Write a **1** next to the picture that comes first.
Write a **2** next to the picture that is next.
Write a **3** next to the last picture.
Color the pictures.

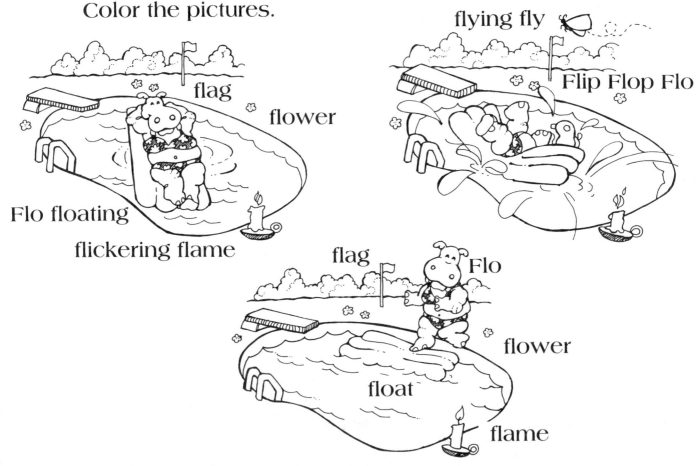

flag
flower
Flo floating
flickering flame

flying fly
Flip Flop Flo

flag
Flo
flower
float
flame

Find some flies on the sticker page.
Put them in the pictures.

fl

Use these words to finish the puzzle.

→ flag
  floor

↓ flower
  fly

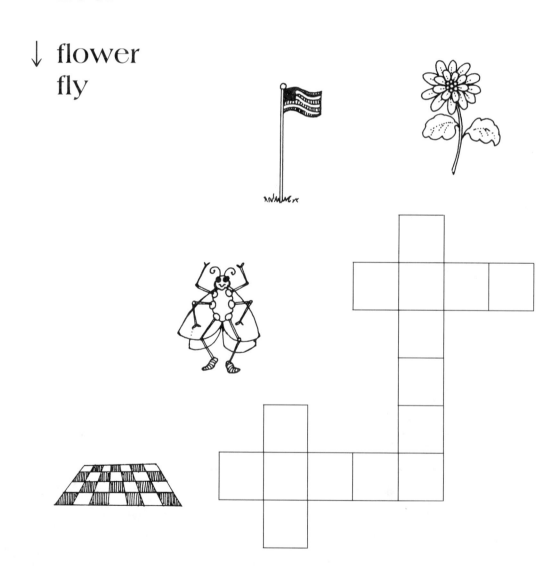

 **st** **star stamp**

Read the title aloud.
Say the first sound in the word **star.**
Write:

_____

stɑr

Follow the path from START to STOP.

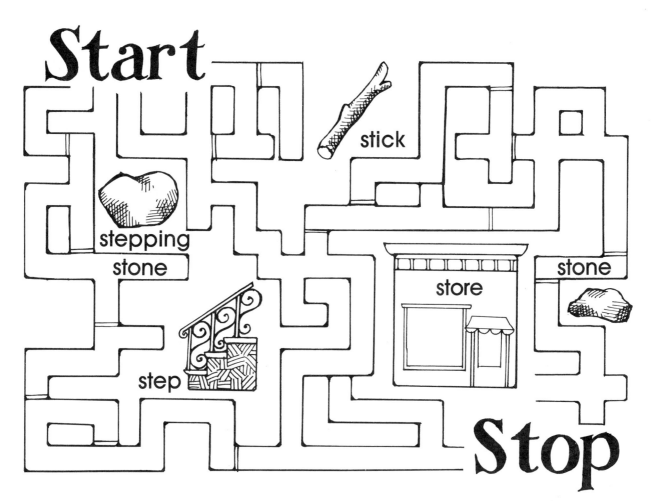

Start

stick

stepping
stone

step

store

stone

Stop

Did you do a good job?
Find a star sticker.
Put it at the top of the page.

Yahoo

DYNOMITE

TERRIFIC!!!

f1

first
prize

GOOD
JOB

#1

blue
blob

NEAT

NICE
WORK

fantastic!
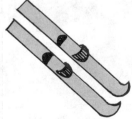
HOT
STUFF

dr

Write **st** on each line to complete the word.

___amp ___ar ___ick ___one

Draw a line from each thing to the place where it belongs in the store.

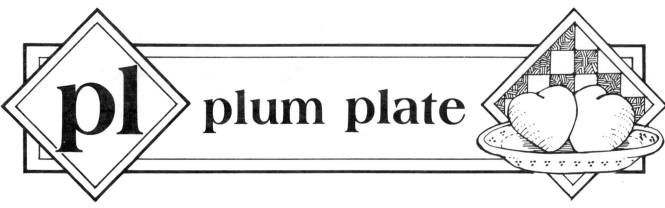

pl plum plate

Read the title aloud.
Say the first sound in the word **plate**.
Write:

plate

Find two plants that are the same.
Draw a circle around each of them.

plant

Please pass the plate.

platypus

plate

plane

Find a fruit sticker that begins with the same sound
as the word plant. Put it on the plate.

One picture in each row has a name that starts with
the same sound as the word **place**.
Draw a circle around it.
Write **pl** to complete each word. Read the word.

frog	plane	cat	sun	___ane
fan	plant	moon	duck	___ant
plate	apple	door	bat	___ate
clock	planet	doll	flower	___anet

Skill: sound/symbol relationship for pl

br

bride
braid

Read the title aloud.
Say the first sound in the word **braid.**
Write:

braid

Find all the things in the picture that start with the same sound as the word **bread**. Color them in.

braid

branches

bracelet

brush

bride

broom

Did you find all the things?
Find a sticker that starts with the same sound as the word **broom**.
Put it at the top of the page.

Use a brown crayon to color all the words that start with the same sound as the word bread.
What did you make?
Find the sticker word.
Put it here:

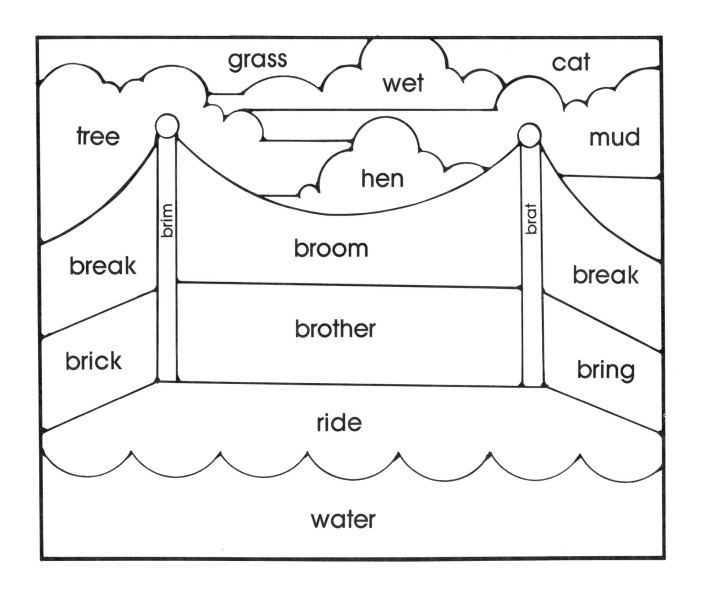

dr

dragon drum

Read the title aloud.
Say the first sound in the word **dragon**.
Write:

dragon

The dragon is dreaming about a drum.
Color the dreaming dragon.
Draw a drum here:

dreaming dragon

Find a dress on the sticker page.
Put it on the dragon who is awake.

Write **dr** to complete each word.
Read the sentences.
Draw a line from each sentence to the matching picture.

The ____agon is ____inking.

The ____agon is ____essing.

Find this sticker.

The ____agon is ____iving.

The ____agon is ____awing.

gr

grapes
grasshopper

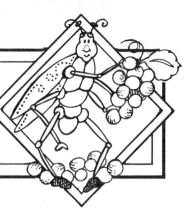

Read the title aloud.
Say the first sound in the word **grapes**.
Write: _____

grapes

Find ten grapes in the picture.
Color the grapes green.

grandfather

greeting

grandchild

grass

ground

Find a sticker word that starts with the same sound
as the word grapes.
Put it at the top of the page.

Greg would like you to make a group of words that start with the same sound as his name.
Find the six words in the list below that begin with **gr**.
Write them on the lines inside this great big grape.
Say each word as you write it.

grape
sheep
me
green
grade
plane

good
grow
ground
sled
child
gray

_____
_____
_____
_____
_____
_____

Write **gr** on each line to complete the words.
Read the sentences below.

My ____andmother is ____eat!

What ____ade are you in?

____ace is ____owing.

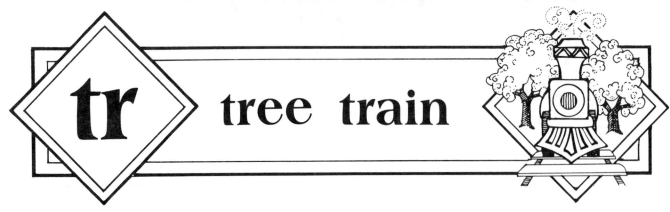

tr tree train

Read the title aloud.
Say the first sound in the word **tree.**
Write: _____

tree - - - - - - - -

Follow the numbers to find Tracey's trunk.
Color the things that start with the same sound as tree.

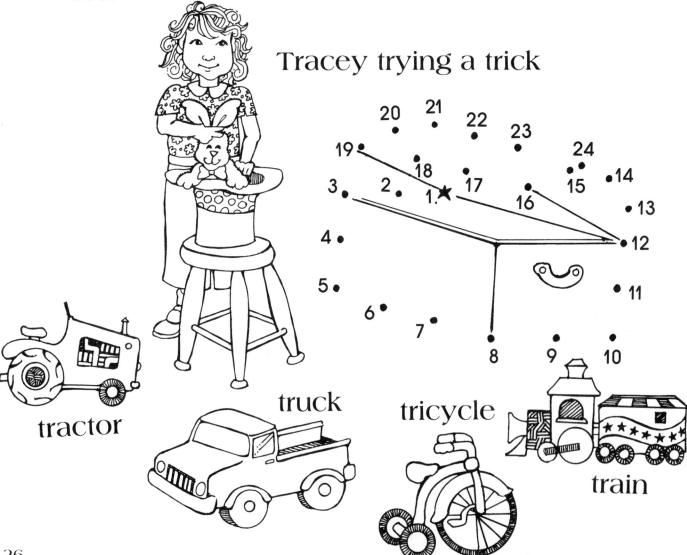

Tracey trying a trick

tractor

truck

tricycle

train

Use these words to finish the puzzle.

→ tractor
↓ truck
  tree
  trunk

plane
cane

Read the title aloud.
That is the long **a** sound.
When you put the letter **e** at the end of some words
the first vowel says its name.
Say these words:
mad   man   plan   can
Write an **e** on each line to make the long **a** sound.

mad_   man_   plan_   can_

Now say the new words.

Find a cane, a mane, and some tape in the picture.
Color them in.

Find a cap and a cape on the sticker page.
Put them on the lion.

28

Skill: recognizing long a; use of silent e

Pete

Read the title aloud.
That is the long **e** sound.

Follow the leashes in Pete's hand to find out which one leads to Pete's pet.
Color Pete's pet.

i

nice
mice

Read the title aloud.
That is the long **i** sound.

Say these words:
dim   hid   fin
Write an **e** on each line to make the long **i** sound.

dim_   hid_   fin_

Now say the new words.
Tim has a new kit.
Follow the numbers to see what
his kit will be.
Color the picture.

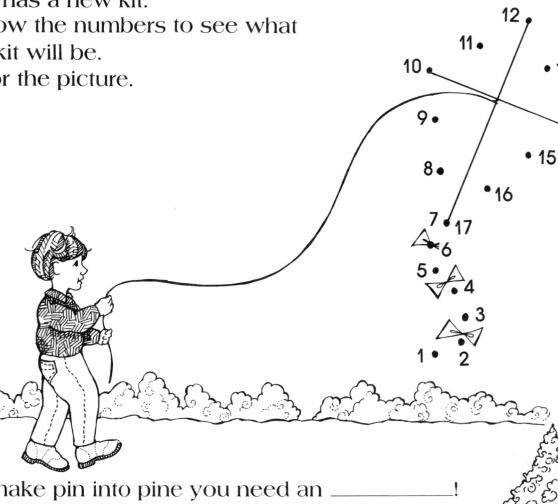

To make pin into pine you need an _____!
Find the letter on the sticker page.

30

Skill: recognizing long i; use of silent e

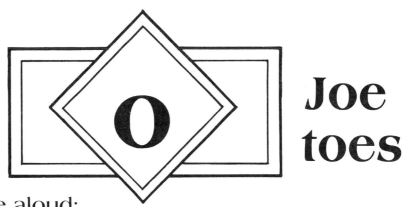

o

Joe
toes

Read the title aloud:
That is the long **o** sound.

Say these words:
not hop mop ton
Write an **e** on each line to make the long **o** sound.

not_ hop_ mop_ ton_

Now say the new words.
Color the two ice cream cones that are exactly the same.

The dog needs a treat.
Find a bone on the sticker page and give it to the dog.

u

mule
flute

Read the title aloud.
That is the long **u** sound.

Say these words:
cut   tub   cub
Write an **e** on each line to make the long **u** sound.

cut__   tub__   cub__

Now say the new words.

Take the cub to the cube.
Write an **e** on each line as you go.

Skill: recognizing long u; use of silent e